"Christians are pressed by very real questions. How does Scripture structure a church, order worship, organize ministry, and define biblical leadership? Those are just examples of the questions that are answered clearly, carefully, and winsomely in this new series from 9Marks. I am so thankful for this ministry and for its incredibly healthy and hopeful influence in so many faithful churches. I eagerly commend this series."

R. Albert Mohler Jr., President, The Southern Baptist Theological Seminary

"Sincere questions deserve thoughtful answers. If you're not sure where to start in answering these questions, let this series serve as a diving board into the pool. These minibooks are winsomely to-the-point and great to read together with one friend or one hundred friends."

Gloria Furman, author, *Missional Motherhood* and *The Pastor's Wife*

"As a pastor, I get asked lots of questions. I'm approached by unbelievers seeking to understand the gospel, new believers unsure about next steps, and maturing believers wanting help answering questions from their Christian family, friends, neighbors, or coworkers. It's in these moments that I wish I had a book to give them that was brief, answered their questions, and pointed them in the right direction for further study. Church Questions is a series that provides just that. Each booklet tackles one question in a biblical, brief, and practical manner. The series may be called Church Questions, but it could be called 'Church Answers.' I intend to pick these up by the dozens and give them away regularly. You should too."

Juan R. Sanchez, Senior Pastor, High Pointe Baptist Church, Austin, Texas

"Where can we Christians find reliable answers to our common questions about life together at church—without having to plow through long, expensive books? The Church Questions booklets meet our need with answers that are biblical, thoughtful, and practical. For pastors, this series will prove a trustworthy resource for guiding church members toward deeper wisdom and stronger unity."

Ray Ortlund, President, Renewal Ministries

How Can I Begin to Teach the Bible?

Church Questions

How Can
I Begin to
Teach the Bible?

David Helm

CROSSWAY®

WHEATON, ILLINOIS

How Can I Begin to Teach the Bible?

© 2024 by 9Marks

Published by Crossway
1300 Crescent Street
Wheaton, Illinois 60187

Cover image and design: Jordan Singer

First printing 2024

Printed in the United States of America

Trade paperback ISBN: 978-1-4335-9147-1
ePub ISBN: 978-1-4335-9149-5
PDF ISBN: 978-1-4335-9148-8

Library of Congress Cataloging-in-Publication Data

Names: Helm, David R., 1961- author.
Title: How can I begin to teach the Bible? / David Helm.
Description: Wheaton, IL : Crossway, 2024. | Series: Church questions | Includes bibliographical references and index.
Identifiers: LCCN 2023052768 (print) | LCCN 2023052769 (ebook) | ISBN 9781433591471 (trade paperback) | ISBN 9781433591488 (pdf) | ISBN 9781433591495 (epub)
Subjects: LCSH: Bible--Study and teaching.
Classification: LCC BS600.3 .H453 2024 (print) | LCC BS600.3 (ebook) | DDC 220.076--dc23/eng/20240213
LC record available at https://lccn.loc.gov/2023052768
LC ebook record available at https://lccn.loc.gov/2023052769

Crossway is a publishing ministry of Good News Publishers.

BP		33	32	31	30	29	28	27	26	25	24
15	14	13	12	11	10	9	8	7	6	5	4	3	2	1

Do your best to present yourself to God as one approved, a worker who has no need to be ashamed, rightly handling the word of truth.

2 Timothy 2:15

This book is for anyone who wants to teach the Bible but doesn't know how to begin. It's also for those who are already teaching the Bible but don't know if they are doing it well.

If either of those statements describes you, you're not alone. Those of us who teach the Bible vocationally have all had to start somewhere. I began teaching the Bible long before I had any thoughts of giving my life to teaching it. I simply fell in love with Jesus and found myself telling others about what I was learning from God's word. But I had no idea if my preparation process or teaching was any good. I just began teaching and preaching—driven along by my desire to put the truth of God's word before the people I knew and loved.

What's your story?

Has a desire to teach the Bible suddenly taken hold of your mind and heart? Did your pastor ask you to consider leading a Bible study? Are you about to give a one-off talk to some youth or campus ministry? One man in my church began teaching the Bible in prison after coming to Christ while being incarcerated!

Whatever has you currently leaning into the task of teaching the Bible, I'm glad you picked up this little book. I want to point you to a well-worn path of wisdom that can guide you on the road to giving Bible talks that are based on (1) sound *principles*, (2) good *preparation*, and (3) pleasing *presentation*.

So let's get started.

———

Part 1: Principles

You Need Confidence

Let me tell you about the first time I prepared a talk from the Bible for a relatively large group of people.

I was eighteen; it had been a year since I had submitted my life to the gospel and fallen in love with Jesus. My public high school of roughly twelve hundred students had recently voted to select two graduating students to speak at commencement. Somehow, I was selected (clearly the criteria had not been being the class valedictorian).

When word got out that I had been selected to speak not everyone was pleased. A few faculty members and classmates even tried to have me removed from the schedule. Why the opposition? Well, I had spent my entire senior year telling just about anyone who would listen about Jesus. And now, a few individuals feared that I would take this opportunity—at commencement of all places—to do it again.

Still, I knew I wanted to say something meaningful to our class from the Bible. A lot was at stake. About three hundred of us were graduating, many of whom were not Christians and another seven hundred or more family members and friends would be in attendance. Given the situation, I knew I needed to speak with sensitivity, so I made it a point to spend time in prayer as I prepared my talk (and my mom was praying too!).

But as commencement drew near I was thrown for a loop. I heard through the grapevine that if I even so much as mentioned the Bible or spoke about Jesus some of my classmates were going to walk out in protest. That gave me pause, not to mention a dose of anxiety. I needed *confidence*—confidence that God would accomplish his purposes through my talk and that the Holy Spirit would overcome my fears.

In the end, I decided to follow through on my desire to say something meaningful to my class from the Bible. I made my way to the lectern—full of fear, yet full of assurance—and encouraged my class to consider three phrases that I hoped would define the student body as we stepped into the future: "Doing justice. Loving kindness. And walking humbly." If you're a student of the Bible, you'll recognize that those three phrases come right out of Micah 6:8.

As I approached my conclusion, no one had given any signs of objecting to my "Bible talk" on justice, kindness, and humility. I closed by mentioning that these words appeared together in the Bible. I then explained that doing justice, loving kindness, and walking with humility were all things that the prophet Micah instructs us to do "with your God." At that point, I pivoted to Jesus as the one we all need if we're going to have any hope of fulfilling God's understanding of justice, kindness, and humility.

As I talked about Jesus, I began to hear the loud sounds of footsteps falling on the wooden bleachers. Some family members and friends of our class were walking out. I still have the cassette recording that captures the stomping of those who exited the gymnasium.

That said, not a single one of my classmates left. In that tension-filled moment, my classmates were all decidedly kind to me, just as I had tried to do my best to be sensitive but loving toward them. I still feel today as I did then: that to truly love people we must tell them about Jesus.

As I reflect on that experience now, over forty years later, I'm deeply aware that whatever faithfulness I may have expressed in those moments was rooted in *confidence*—not confidence in myself, confidence in God's word.

If you're just getting started teaching the Bible, that's the first thing I want to put in your mind: beginning preachers and teachers (and experienced ones too!) need confidence in God's word.

Anyone who is going to teach the Bible needs real conviction that God acts through the proclamation of his word. Additionally, you need confidence in the Holy Spirit. You need to trust that the Spirit can overcome any opposition to his word in the hearts of your hearers and you need to trust that he can empower you to overcome any fear you may have in proclaiming his word.

You Need Right Convictions

Teaching the Bible well starts with confidence in God's word. But you also need a set of godly *convictions*. Three particular convictions are a good start: (1) the Bible is God's word, (2) prayer is a must, and (3) the local church is one of God's greatest gifts.

Conviction 1: The Bible is God's word. Having right convictions about the Bible is essential to teaching it faithfully.

To illustrate what I mean let's take a look at some *ART*:

A (author)
R (reader)
T (text)

If you're going to teach the Bible faithfully you need to understand *ART*, that is, you need to understand how the authors (A) of the text

(T) of Scripture relate to the readers (R) of Scripture.

Some Bible teachers mistakenly believe that the text (T) of Scripture is nothing more than a collection of human writings. They think the Bible only provides us with a centuries-old "history of God." Other teachers believe that God had a hand in writing the Bible, but that over time human hands corrupted it. As a result readers (R) must discover God's message for us in Scripture by separating the wheat of truth from the chaff of error. In other words, it's up to the readers (R) to establish what the Bible really says.

But do you see the problem with that line of reasoning? If you treat the Bible as a mixed bag of truth and error, then you're really not submitting to its authority because *you* can always discount or ignore any parts that challenge or trouble you. Unless you're convinced that the Bible is God's word, then the reader (R) of the text (T) is the final authority on what the Bible says and what the author (A) has to teach us.

In contrast, the Bible asserts that it is nothing less than the authoritative, inerrant word of God: "All Scripture is breathed out by God and profitable for teaching, for reproof, for correction, and for training in righteousness" (2 Tim. 3:16).

Faithful Bible teachers should believe what Scripture says about itself:

- God is Scripture's ultimate author (A).
- Therefore, the original text (T) is inerrant, authoritative, and infallible.
- Therefore, we the readers (R) are never free to ignore any part of Scripture or find meanings in Scripture which simply aren't there.

To put it differently, your conviction needs to be that the authors (A) were carried along by the Spirit of God (2 Pet. 1:21), that the text (T) has not been corrupted, and that the reader (R) must only teach what accords with the sound doctrine of the author's intention.

By way of encouragement, let me suggest to you that in my experience those who share these beliefs become the types of people God uses to win men and women to faith in Jesus and to build up the body of Christ.

If you're going to teach Scripture well, you need to hold the conviction that you're teaching nothing less than God's authoritative, inerrant word.

Conviction 2: Prayer is a must. Faithful Bible teachers not only believe that the Bible is God's word, they believe in the necessity of prayer—both for their *preparation* and their *presentation.*

Certainly, ordinary reading strategies will help you understand God's word. But spiritual things are spiritually discerned (1 Cor. 2:14). We must depend on the ministry of the Holy Spirit to properly understand the Bible. If the Spirit does not give us understanding, even the best presentation will never be able to make up for our ignorance.

If anything good comes out of our teaching ministry, it's not because we're so gifted and clever. God's word and Spirit are producing the spiritual fruit. In fact, I have seen God do wonderful things even when my own exegesis was flawed and my presentation was faulty. As Bible teachers demonstrate a reliance on God in prayer, God honors their hard work with the attending power of his Spirit.

Before you even begin the preparation process, prayer must come first. In my life, I ask God to help me understand the passage. I ask him to help me submit my life to everything that I discover while studying his word. Further, I ask him to work powerfully in my presentation. I would encourage you to join me in this conviction and in these prayers. Exhibit humility before God by living out the conviction that prayer is a must.

Conviction 3: The local church is one of God's greatest gifts. Often someone has the desire to teach the Bible before ever having an opportunity to do so. Like most things in life, aspiration precedes action. That said, an aspiring Bible teacher shouldn't ever set out on his own. Charting your own course simply based on your desires and aspirations is spiritually dangerous.

You need a local church.

The local church formally recognizes us as belonging to Christ and teaches us to obey everything that Jesus commanded. The local church is where we witness God's word faithfully taught by pastors who are "able to teach" (1 Tim. 3:2). It's also the place where we see obedience to God's word modeled.

If you want to know how to begin teaching the Bible, the local church is the school in which you are trained. After all Christ established local churches to be the pillar and buttress of the truth (1 Tim. 3:15). So if you desire to teach, you need to be nurtured in a local church under the authority of godly elders. Specifically, the local church is essential for your growth as a teacher because it both (1) *assesses* your competence and (2) *appoints* you to teaching roles.

Think about your need for *assessment*. When I went to college, I got involved in a wonderful, Bible-teaching church. The pastoral staff took an interest in me, and eventually I did an internship under the associate pastor. He put me to work and even gave me a few opportunities to teach and lead in some smaller settings. Those opportunities, safely tucked away from the limelight, were invaluable. They allowed me to try my hand at Bible teaching around people who loved me and gave me honest feedback. They told me how to improve and instructed me on how I could handle God's word more faithfully. In short, they *assessed* my readiness to teach the Bible.

But that local church did more than simply assess my abilities. They *appointed* me to the work of teaching. Having helped me develop the ability to teach and having assessed that I was able to effectively handle God's word, they gave me more and more public teaching opportunities and encouraged me to continue in that work.

This church was patient with me, encouraging me along this path even when I failed. I will never forget one of my first sermons in a church service. Kent Hughes was my pastor. He gave me the opportunity to preach, even as he sat in the pews listening attentively. From the response I had gotten from friends and congregants, I thought I had done quite well.

A few days later, Kent invited me into his office to provide some feedback. I will never forget what he said: "David, that was a fine sermon, and helpful to many. But I couldn't help but feel that you didn't quite tell us what the text was actually trying to convey." Looking back on it, that hour with him was incredibly formative. Rather than being discouraged, it lit a fire under me to develop and grow. I wanted to make progress—and the local church was my greatest gift in doing so.

I want that for you too! So join a healthy, gospel-believing church that teaches the Bible. Don't ask to teach a Bible study on day one. Start serving the church and encouraging people with Scripture in whatever informal opportunities the Lord provides. Submit yourself to the elders and ask them to *assess* your preaching and teaching gifts. Don't be a self-appointed teacher. Look for the church and its leaders to give you teaching opportunities at the right time. Wait patiently for them to *appoint* you to preach or teach. A mentoring relationship in the context of the local church is indispensable to discerning if the role of Bible teacher is right for you.

Now that your *confidence* is in the right place and you've got the right *convictions*, you are ready to get started.

You've got a "Bible talk" coming up. So what should your preparation look like?

What follows is a step-by-step guide that will lead you from preparation to presentation. I've tried to describe a process that can be carried out in roughly 10 hours (though that may vary depending on your experience and skill level). Let's get started.

Part 2: Preparation

Preparation involves three primary steps: (1) find the structure and emphasis, (2) understand the context, and (3) highlight the message of the gospel.

Step 1: Find the Structure and Emphasis

Beginning Bible teachers often begin their preparation time asking, "What can I say from this text?" Don't do that! That question will ensure you'll be more concerned about filling time rather than getting the message of the text.

Let me suggest a better first step. I would like to introduce it to you with a drawing, followed by a true story.

Meet *Perry Mastodon*.

Perry Mastodon

In October of 1963, Federal Court Judge Joseph Perry decided to dig a pond in his backyard. As backhoes began to excavate the land, their digging unearthed a massive bone. Local scientists immediately took interest and escorted the oversized discovery to Chicago's renowned Field Museum of Natural History. They eventually determined the bone belonged to an extinct animal, and Judge Perry's backyard became an archeological dig. In the end, experts uncovered 115 bones from this ancient beast. Even without all the bones, scientists were able to determine, the *shape* of the skeletal structure. Perry's backyard had been the home of a mastodon. Or, as it is still sometimes referred to, a *Perry Mastodon.*

What's my point?

Just as scientists unearthed enough bones to identify the skeletal structure of the mastodon, Bible teachers must study the text to uncover its structure. We need to know how our text "fits together." We need to understand the *shape* of the text.

Every biblical text has its own divinely inspired literary *shape.* That shape (or structure) reveals the Spirit's divinely intended *emphasis*— it reveals the argument the author of Scripture is making. Your job, like a good paleontologist, is to discover it!

So how do you do that?

First, you need to recognize that the Bible is composed of different *types* of literature:

- narrative
- discourse
- poetry

Or as I like to think of them:

- story (narrative)
- speech (discourse)
- song (poetry)

Each one of these *types* of literature in the Bible requires different reading strategies. Story tellers organize their material differently than speech or song writers. We, of course, intuitively recognize this fact: we read love poems differently from campaign speeches and recipes differently from novels.

So you first need to determine what type of literature you are studying: Are you reading a story (like an Old Testament narrative or a Gospel), a speech (like one of Paul's letters), or a song (like a Psalm)? Once you've determined your text's type, you'll be able to use the most effective tools for digging out its structure.

Here are some strategies to get you started.

The shape and emphasis of a *story* often revolve around a plot—complete with a setting, conflict, rising tension, climax, resolution, and new setting. See if you can trace the arc of the story's plot by asking questions like:

- What is the setting of the story?
- What conflict is at the center of the story?
- How does the author show rising tension, or how does the conflict develop?
- What's the climax of the story?
- How did the story resolve?
- What's the new setting (or situation) for the characters at the end of the story?

Look for ways the author might identify major sections in the story through things like scene changes, temporal markers, or changes in location. These tools will help you begin to see the way the author has put the parts together.

Speech writers shape their material from the bones of basic grammar. If you are preparing to teach from an epistle you can unearth its skeletal structure by looking for the main subject, the verbs, and by paying special attention to things like commands, prepositions, and conjunctions. You'll want to pay special attention to words like "because," "for this reason," or "therefore." Your goal is to follow the author's argument and see what he's trying to teach his readers.

For poetry, or *song*, try to notice how the writer develops images and ideas. Think about Psalm 1. The literary shape and emphasis is tied to contrasting images: a fruit-bearing tree and chaff driven away by the wind. These images are connected to the ideas of the righteous and the wicked, the blessed and the cursed, and the destinies of both on the final day of judgment.

So much more could be said on how to excavate your text to uncover its divinely intended *structure* and *emphasis*. But in a book of this length, that's simply not possible. I would encourage you to visit simeontrust.org and register for the *First Principles* course. That resource will not only help you learn how to discern a text's structure, it will also help you with all the preparation steps I'm about to outline.

Find the structure, that's step 1. Any time you teach the Bible you need to understand the text's *emphasis* by uncovering its inspired *structure*.

How long should that take? That depends on your experience and the difficulty of your passage. Usually, I spend an hour working out the structure of a passage. Set a modest goal for yourself and don't get discouraged if it takes you a long time. You'll get better with more practice. Ask pastors or disciplers who are experienced at handling God's word to help you.

Step 2: Understand the Context

After spending some time trying to understand the structure and emphasis of the text you're teaching, I would encourage you to spend the next two hours of preparation focusing on *context*. Let me be clear: by context, I do not mean the context of *your* audience. I mean the context of your passage, the context of the author, and the context of the audience to whom your passage was originally written—that's what you need to focus on in step 2.

You need to consider the *historical, literary, biblical,* and *cultural* contexts of your passage.

These four contexts are like four prongs that hold the diamond in an engagement ring.

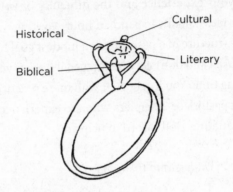

Engagement Ring of Contexts

Just as four prongs secure a precious stone in a particular setting, understanding the four contexts of a passage of Scripture helps us uphold the beauty and glory of that particular text.

So let's get some definitions in place. What do we mean by *historical, literary, biblical,* and *cultural* context?

Historical context refers to the situation and circumstances of those to whom the text was written, as well as those of the author. Ask questions like: When was this written? What was going on at the time both in the church and in the world? How do my answers to those questions influence my understanding of the passage?

Literary context refers to what the author says before and after the text you're studying. You particularly want to consider the questions: What argument has the author made up to this point? How does my passage contribute to that larger argument? How do later passages in this book develop that same point?

Biblical context refers to any citations of or allusions to earlier Scripture. Ask questions like: Does my text quote any earlier parts of Scripture? Does it develop any ideas or doctrines found in other parts of Scripture? Does my passage allude to any earlier Scripture and if so why?

Cultural context refers to the ancient culture of the author and his original audience. Cultural context makes sense of any details in the text that would have been understood by the author, but not necessarily by our audience. Ask questions like: Are there any customs or traditions from that culture which might help me understand my passage? Are there things mentioned in my passage that need to be explained because they reflect unfamiliar customs or ways of thinking?

Understanding each of these contexts is essential for sound preparation. Consider allotting 30 minutes of study to each context. Don't try to be comprehensive. You can always revisit each context if you have extra time. Plus, you'll get better at understanding each context with each lesson you teach.

I can't overstate the value of devoting attention to context early in your preparation. Context controls our understanding of the text. It keeps us focused on what the biblical authors are actually saying, rather than using the text in ways that would have been unrecognizable to the original author. Again, these different contexts are like prongs on a ring—they fix the gemstone of your passage in place. Or, to use a different metaphor, the various contexts function like iron railroad tracks that keep you on the rails of biblical fidelity.

One note of caution before we move on: far too many preachers and Bible teachers overuse the many interesting contextual details when they present their lesson. I call these kind of Bible teachers "Prong Preachers." They cram everything they learned about context into their lessons, instead of focusing on how the context informs their understanding of the text itself. Remember, understanding context is supposed to help you put the glories of your text on display, not the other way around.

Step 3: Highlight the Gospel

By this point in your preparation, you've probably invested three to four hours of study. But you still have more work to do. Every good Bible teacher will want his hearers to understand the relationship between his text and the gospel.

That means *you* need to know how your passage highlights the gospel.

The life, death, and resurrection of Jesus Christ is the unifying center of Scripture. Everything in the Old Testament anticipates or points to Jesus. Similarly everything in the New Testament reflects, or looks back on, Jesus's person and work. Jesus himself affirmed this reality. He taught that all Scripture pointed to him (Luke 24:25–27, 44–47)—as did the apostles (Rom. 1:1–6; 2 Pet. 1:19–21).

The principle looks like this:

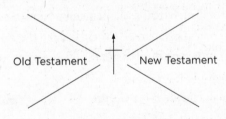

Old Testament   New Testament

Christ as the Unifying Center of Scripture

When it comes to highlighting the gospel, Bible teachers generally fall into one of two errors. *The first error is to neglect Jesus altogether.*

Renowned nineteenth-century Baptist preacher Charles Spurgeon put it this way:

> We should know Jesus, for we have the Scriptures to reflect His image, and yet how possible it is for us to open that precious book and have no glimpse of the Wellbeloved? Dear child of God, are you in that state? Jesus feedeth among the lilies of the word, and you walk among those lilies, and yet you behold him not. He is accustomed to walk through the glades of Scripture, and to commune with His people, as the Father did with Adam in the cool of the day, and you are in the garden of Scripture, but cannot see Him, though He is always there.[1]

Let's look at an example of how this happens. Imagine someone in your church has been tasked with teaching a Bible study on 1 Timothy 1:1–2:

> Paul, an apostle of Christ Jesus by command of God our Savior and of Christ Jesus our hope.
>
> To Timothy, my true child in the faith:

Grace, mercy, and peace from God the Father and Christ Jesus our Lord.

Following step 1, the Bible teacher unearths the *structure* of the passage. He quickly discerns that this passage has three "bones" that organize the material:

- 1:1 reveals Paul, the author
- 1:2a gives us Timothy, the audience
- 1:2b tell us about Paul's hopes for Timothy

Now he moves on to step 2: *context*. He studies Paul's conversion and call to ministry. He knows how Paul and Timothy met. He learns some things about the city of Ephesus—the place where Timothy pastored. He also takes note of the fact that Paul's hopes for Timothy are very similar to his desires for churches in his other letters.

With this knowledge in hand, the Bible teacher sets out to deliver a three-point message. In the first point he has a lot to say about the apostle Paul, in the second he has a lot to say about Timothy, and finally he explains Paul's hopes for Timothy.

So far so good.

But imagine at this point the Bible teacher decides his work is done. He stands up and explains these two verses in context in a three-point lesson (1) Paul the apostle; (2) Timothy his protégé; and (3) Paul's hopes for Timothy.

But there's one big problem.

The lesson I just described doesn't say anything about Jesus. It hasn't explained the relationship between this text and the gospel— even though Jesus is mentioned *three times* in these two verses! Take a look: Paul identifies himself as an apostle *of Christ Jesus*, according to the promise of life that is *in Christ Jesus*, and he desires for Timothy things that come *from Christ Jesus*.

Jesus and the gospel are central to each section of this text. All of Scripture ultimately points to or flows from the life, death, and resurrection of Jesus. He is there, in plain sight; we shouldn't ever teach the Bible and omit the gospel.

In light of this, the sermon outline for 1 Timothy 1:1–2 would have been better stated as (1) the calling of Christ upon Paul, and (2) the encouragement of Christ for Timothy.

A second error is to preach Jesus in superficial, predictable ways. Bible teachers make this error when they only speak of Jesus when telling unbelievers to receive the gospel.

I call this kind of Bible teacher a "Punxsutawney Phil Preacher."

Punxsutawney Phil Preacher Groundhog

Let me explain. Each year on February 2, a springtime ritual plays out in Punxsutawney, PA. A city official pulls a groundhog ("Punxsutawney Phil") from his winter hole and, according to folklore, if Phil sees his shadow, then winter will linger on—"six more weeks of the same."

And so it is with some Bible teachers. They are pulled out of their study into the pulpit week by week, only to preach Christ as something tacked on to the end of the sermon when telling unbelievers how they can be right with God. Each and every Sunday, they simply give "six more weeks of the same." As a result, listeners become bored with the preaching, and worse yet, bored with Jesus.

If we say the same thing about Jesus every week, if we reduce the message of the gospel as something that's *only* relevant for unbelievers, then we truncate Christ's beauty and glory.

For instance, you could point to the benefits Christ has for every Christian in 1 Timothy 1:1–2 by highlighting Paul's insistence that Jesus is our hope. You can comfort the Christian listener by reminding them that this same Jesus who supported Timothy will likewise provide all the grace, mercy, and peace we need when we are asked to do difficult things for him.

Good Bible teachers must learn to highlight the beauties of the gospel as they're unfolded in every passage of Scripture. Don't be overly predictable in your teaching about

Jesus. Consider how your text points you to the grace of God found in the person and work of Christ. Consider how the gospel in your passage applies not just to unbelievers but to believers as well. Spend some time in preparation thinking about how to highlight the particular aspects of the gospel that are present in your text. Doing this well is not easy. It will take time and practice.

By this point in your preparation, you've completed three distinct study sessions totaling somewhere between five to six hours. Hopefully the benefit of following this pattern of study is becoming obvious. Your understanding of the structure has revealed the main emphasis of the text. Your time investigating the four contexts has produced a better understanding of the meaning and intention of the text. And now you have a particular aspect of the gospel to highlight from your text.

Now you need to start thinking about *presentation*.

Part 3: Presentation

Eventually you need to "turn the corner" from preparation to presentation.

Augustine wrote,

> There are two things upon which all
> interpretation of Scripture depends:
> the process of discovering what we
> need to learn,
> and the process of presenting what we
> have learnt.[2]

Preparation is the process of discovering what you need to learn about the text. *Presentation* is the process of putting together what you intend to say. The first part involves studying. The second involves writing.

So what do you need to know about presentation?

First, Know Your Goal

In one complete sentence, you should be able to state what you are trying to convince your listeners of from the text you are teaching. Think of it this way: during *preparation* you've given all your attention to the biblical text. But for *presentation*, you need to consider the people to whom you are speaking.

Regrettably, many Bible teachers think that biblical exposition is simply teaching the main point of the passage without ever considering what they're trying to accomplish in the lives of their listeners. They reduce the task of teaching to simply asserting the main point of the passage. As a result, their presentation sounds like little more than a running commentary on the biblical text.

But good Bible teachers understand the difference between simply stating the big idea of the text and establishing an aim for their talk. Consider this point carefully: If you want to effectively teach the Bible you need to recast the main point of the passage so that *your* listeners live under the truth of that main point.

"Turning the corner" from preparation to presentation demands thought and reflection, not more exegesis and research. In fact, much of your time considering presentation should simply look a lot like this:

Auguste Rodin's *The Thinker*

Many folks have at least seen images of Auguste Rodin's *The Thinker*. You can find the original bronze sculpture in Paris. It has quite a storied history. But here's what I want you to learn from *The Thinker*: when it comes to presentation, every good Bible teacher should think long and hard about the *aim* or *goal* of the lesson. This may take me an hour or more. But remember: good Bible teachers linger over the truth of the text, and they *also* linger over the best way to express that truth. They don't just explain, they establish a goal for their hearers.

For instance, recently I preached on Matthew 18:15–20, a well-known text related to church discipline. That said, the goal I had for my congregation was stated this way, "Those who follow Jesus are committed to getting there together."

In sum, you're not ready to preach or teach until you can state the goal your text has for your particular audience. Don't neglect this step, even if it takes you a couple of hours of quiet thought and consideration.

Second, Construct an Outline

Once you have a clearly stated goal, it's time to construct an outline for your talk. The most effective presenters arrange their material in ways that serve their stated goal. Your *arrangement* should strengthen and highlight your *aim*. Ordinarily, constructing an outline might involve a couple of hours of time.

When it comes to constructing an outline for your message, all sermons and Bible talks should follow a normal pattern—an introduction, a body, and a conclusion. You might think of these components simply as a beginning, a middle, and an end.

The Body. The middle section, *the body*, will take up most of the time of your lesson, and I suggest constructing it first. Write out the one thing you want to persuade your listeners of from your text *and the points that prove it.* Those points will make up the body of your lesson.

As you construct the body of your lesson, you'll need to refer constantly to your earlier work that identified the text's *structure.* The relationship between the structural shape and emphasis of your text to the shape and emphasis of your talk can be seen in a simple drawing like the one on the next page.

Mirror One Another

Quite simply, the body of your lesson should resemble the body of the biblical text. The two should *mirror* one another. If the text presents you with two major parts, then your sermon should have two parts. For instance, if you were asked to teach on 1 Samuel 21, your preparation would have uncovered that the text divides into two sections, each marked by a change in location.

- 1 Samuel 21:1–9: David gets supplies in the house of the Lord.
- 1 Samuel 21:10–15: David is safeguarded in the house of his enemy.

When it came time to construct an outline, the body of your message might look something like this:

- 1 Samuel 21:1-9: In Christ, God provides for us.
- 1 Samuel 21:10-15: In Christ, God protects us.[3]

Allow the shape and emphasis of the text to control the shape and emphasis of your talk. In this way, your task is not so much creating outlines, but recasting the organization of the biblical material to meet the needs of your particular audience. Notice also how this outline hardwires a connection to the gospel into the message and its application by saying we receive provision and protection "in Christ."

Establishing clear and simple headers for the body of your talk is essential but not enough. The middle part of your message must also work out how you will convey these truths to your audience. Your points will inevitably raise questions in the minds of your hearers. They will even elicit possible objections that your presentation must take some time to address. As such, good Bible teachers learn to build into the body of their messages what needs to be conceded in order to get a hearing as well as what must be refuted if they are to have any hope of persuading those who hear them.

The Conclusion. After constructing the body of the message, I recommend writing the conclusion. What does a good conclusion do? It forcefully re-articulates your goal in ways that arrest the mind and heart of your listener for obedience to Christ. That's the goal, and there isn't any magic formula to make sure it happens. An illustration or story may help, or it may not. Concluding your talk by returning to the way you began may be best, but not always. And when it comes to length, don't exceed the time it takes to have the weight of the message fall on the mind of your hearers.

One writer put it this way:

The preacher should restrict the length of his conclusion with a severe and jealous hand. Its object is only to place the truth which has been explained or proved in contact with the heart and conscience. Every word which exceeds this is an excrescence. The most important thing, therefore, is that you know when to stop, and that you be sure to stop when you have done.[4]

The Introduction. You are now ready to construct your introduction. A good introduction will accomplish at least three things. (1) You must win the affection of your hearers. Your audience must be put in a frame of mind where they *want* to listen to what you have to say. Don't assume that this is the case. (2) The introduction must state your goal. The audience needs to know what you are driving at and hoping for them. Finally, (3) an introduction should give your audience a sense of how you are going to achieve your goal. Provide some signposts for them that you intend to follow as you move through your message.

One last warning: Bible teachers often have long introductions. Some preachers take up

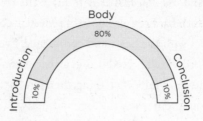

The Sermonic Arc

to ten minutes or more before getting to their text. As a general rule, I suggest limiting your introduction to no more than 10 percent of the total speaking time allotted to you. So if your talk should be twenty minutes, try to get into the body of the message within two. If you have thirty minutes to speak, your introduction should be roughly three minutes. Also, I suggest you allot no more than 10 percent for your conclusion. That leaves a full 80 percent of your time for the body of the talk.

I hope these points on constructing an outline will enable you to teach lessons that are rational, clear, simple, and faithful. Work hard

on the arrangement of your material so that it
serves the argument of your message.

Third, Drive the Truth Home

Good Bible teachers aren't content with their
talks unless their messages aim at transforming
the lives of those who listen. They want to drive
the truth home. And for that, our presentation
must include applications. Here's my drawing
for this principle:

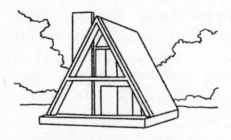

The "A-Frame" for Application

The A-frame house was an architectural
style with a steeply angled roofline that surged
in popularity in the mid-1950s after Andrew

Geller built one on Long Island that was featured in the *New York Times*.

For our purposes, think of the drawing this way: just as an architect creates drawings, which when constructed become a house, so too Bible teachers must design messages *that frame in applications* for listeners to take home with them. And we do so because if our teaching fails to make it home, then our ministry isn't providing life-transforming help.

Regrettably, some Bible teachers don't spend any time on application. They don't think that's their job. "After all," they claim, "isn't the Holy Spirit the one who enlightens us, empowers us, and enables us to live out the truths of God's word?" While that may be true, those truths shouldn't alleviate the preacher from driving home the truths of God's word.

So how do we do apply God's word?

First, your applications should always be derived from the aim of the biblical author and therefore your applications should serve your stated goal for your hearers. One way to visualize the role of application in your message is to think of it as an adhesive. An adhesive is a substance that you "apply" to one object to affix it to another. Your application is essentially endeavoring to glue the truths of God's word to the lives of your listeners. You want the contention of the biblical author to adhere to the conduct of your audience.

Second, applications stick better if you connect them to the images of the biblical text. For instance, if the text presents truths with an agricultural metaphor, your applications will land better if you select illustrations, quotes, or stories from the same. If your applications mirror the metaphors of the text, you have a better chance of driving the truth home.

Finally, don't use applications for the sake of entertainment. Use them to edify and evangelize. Sometimes teachers seem more concerned about getting a laugh than helping their listeners grow in Christ. Humor is good, even essential for good communication. But our aim shouldn't ever be to get a laugh. Our aim should be to help people grow in the grace and knowledge of Christ.

Let's sum up. How should you think about presentation: (1) know your goal, (2) construct your outline, and (3) drive the truth of the text home with solid applications.

Now Go Get Started

"How do I begin teaching the Bible?" More could be said. Indeed, more *should* be said. But in a primer this size, I hope I've given you enough to start. I've provided you with a pathway that can be successfully navigated in about ten hours. Many talks will take more preparation than that. And for teachers who plan to speak from a complete manuscript the journey will undoubtedly take longer.

From the outset, my prayer for this little book is that God will use it to strengthen his church and that many who desire to teach the Bible will understand what it takes to do it well. If, after reading this book, your desire to teach the Bible is still strong, I would encourage you to have a conversation with your pastor. You won't find a better person to help you process what you are learning along the way.

Notes

1. Charles Spurgeon, *Evening by Evening* (London: Passmore and Alabaster, 1868), 305.
2. Augustine, *On Christian Teaching*, trans. R. H. Green (Oxford: Oxford University Press; 1997), 9.
3. See—not every sermon has to have three points!
4. Robert L. Dabney, *Evangelical Eloquence: A Course of Lectures on Preaching* (Edinburgh: Banner of Truth, 1999), 177–78.

Scripture Index

IX 9Marks

Building Healthy Churches

9Marks exists to equip church leaders with a biblical vision and practical resources for displaying God's glory to the nations through healthy churches.

To that end, we want to see churches characterized by these nine marks of health:

1. Expositional Preaching
2. Gospel Doctrine
3. A Biblical Understanding of Conversion and Evangelism
4. Biblical Church Membership
5. Biblical Church Discipline
6. A Biblical Concern for Discipleship and Growth
7. Biblical Church Leadership
8. A Biblical Understanding of the Practice of Prayer
9. A Biblical Understanding and Practice of Missions

Find all our Crossway titles and other resources at 9Marks.org.

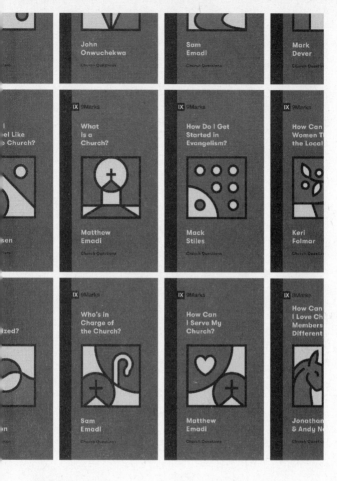

IX **9Marks** Church Questions

Providing ordinary Christians with sound and
accessible biblical teaching by answering
common questions about church life.

For more information, visit crossway.org.